Composition of Matter

Morgaine Paris

Consultant

Trent Nash, M.S.E.
Aerospace Engineer

Publishing Credits

Rachelle Cracchiolo, M.S.Ed., *Publisher*
Conni Medina, M.A.Ed., *Managing Editor*
Diana Kenney, M.A.Ed., NBCT, *Content Director*
Dona Herweck Rice, *Series Developer*
Robin Erickson, *Multimedia Designer*
Timothy Bradley, *Illustrator*

Image Credits: Cover, pp.1,5, 12, 14, 21, 25 (bottom, 27 iStock; pp.4, 8, 16 Alamy; pp.7, 17 Science Source; p.9 (background) Getty Images; p.11 Richard Kali/Science Source; p.18 (illustration) Grace Le; p.19-20 (illustrations) Monique Dominguez; p.21 (top) Charles D. Winters/ Science Source, (bottom) Andrew Lambert Photography/ Science Source; p.25 (top) DePiep/Wikimedia Commons; all other images from Shutterstock.

Library of Congress Cataloging-in-Publication Data

Paris, Morgaine, author.
 Composition of matter / Morgaine Paris.
  pages cm
 Summary: "Our world is a diverse place. It is covered with growing plants, flowing rivers, and roaring winds. And it's all made of matter. Even you and this book are made of matter. Matter can be broken into tiny pieces. These pieces fit together to shape the world."-- Provided by publisher.
 Audience: Grades 4 to 6
 Includes index.
 ISBN 978-1-4807-4720-3 (pbk.)
1. Matter--Constitution--Juvenile literature.
2. Atomic theory--Juvenile literature.
3. Matter--Properties--Juvenile literature. I. Title.
 QC173.16.P35 2016
 539.7--dc23
                    2015002695

Teacher Created Materials

5301 Oceanus Drive
Huntington Beach, CA 92649-1030
http://www.tcmpub.com

ISBN 978-1-4807-4720-3
© 2016 Teacher Created Materials, Inc.

Table of Contents

Through a Chemist's Eyes

Look around you. What do you see? Maybe you see a book, a dog, or a tree. Maybe you're staring at your hands or your clothes. What do all of these things have in common? For one thing, they're all made of matter.

Matter, in and of itself, is a pretty simple concept. In physics, matter is defined as anything that has mass and takes up space. But what does that mean exactly?

Matter is everywhere. It is anything that can be touched, moved, or interacted with physically. Pretty much anything that can be described as "stuff" is matter. Trees and dogs are made of matter. You and this book are made of matter. Even the air around you is made of matter.

But what else do people, trees, and air have in common? They're all composed, or made up, of tiny microscopic pieces called *atoms*. These atoms are unimaginably small. In fact, there are more atoms in a single grain of sand than the estimated number of stars in the Milky Way—about fifty thousand times more. That's an awful lot of pieces!

There is also a whole branch of science devoted to studying these tiny bits of matter—chemistry. Dive in and see the world through a chemist's eyes.

In 1803, chemist John Dalton said that all matter is made of atoms. It's called the *atomic theory*.

John Dalton

gold

Properties

Properties are how we recognize things. We know gold is a soft, yellow metal. *Soft, yellow,* and *metal* are properties of gold. Size and mass are also properties. Anything you observe about a substance is a kind of property.

Gold can be melted. This is another of its properties.

 Don't trust atoms—they make up everything. Ha-ha, get it?

Inside an Atom

    The concept that everything is made of tiny pieces isn't new. Ancient Greek scientists believed everything was made up of tiny indestructible balls. As it turns out, they weren't exactly right. The atoms we know today aren't ball-shaped, solid, or indestructible. In fact, atoms are made up of even smaller pieces, or particles, called *subatomic particles*. *Subatomic* means they are smaller than atoms. These particles include **protons**, **neutrons**, and **electrons**.

    Protons and neutrons are both found in the center, or **nucleus**, of an atom. Protons and neutrons have about the same mass. Electrons are located outside of the nucleus. Compared to protons and neutrons, electrons are tiny! The mass of an electron is about 1/2,000th the mass of a proton or neutron. Because of this, the mass of the nucleus accounts for nearly the entire mass of the atom. But there is something else surprising about the way an atom is put together. The diameter of the nucleus is about 1/100,000th of that of an atom as a whole. That's right, the largest pieces take up the least amount of space!

If an atom were enlarged to the size of a sports arena, its nucleus would be around the size of a pea.

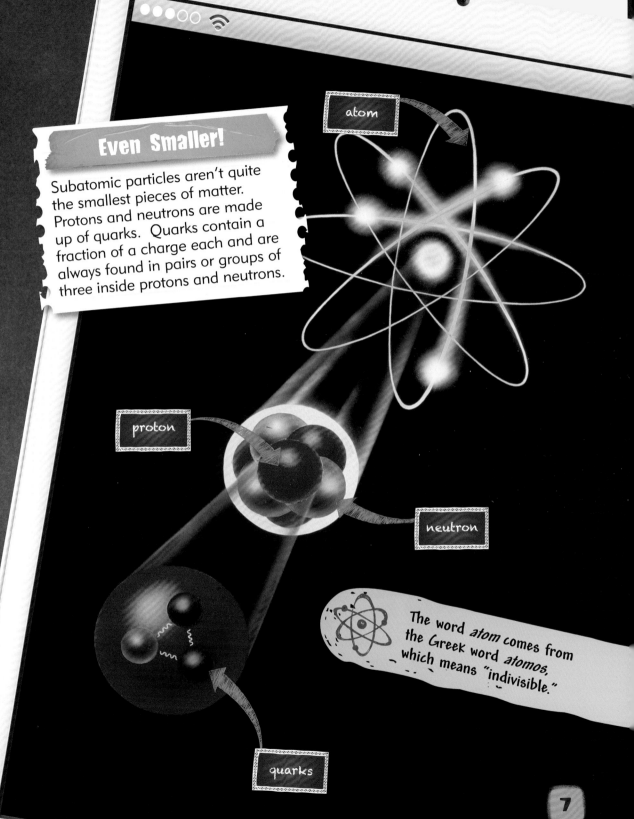

Even Smaller!

Subatomic particles aren't quite the smallest pieces of matter. Protons and neutrons are made up of quarks. Quarks contain a fraction of a charge each and are always found in pairs or groups of three inside protons and neutrons.

atom

proton

neutron

The word *atom* comes from the Greek word *atomos*, which means "indivisible."

quarks

How is this even possible? It's because of the way subatomic particles are arranged in the atom.

Neutrons and protons are bound together very tightly in the nucleus. They are quite difficult to move or break apart. But electrons are always in motion. They buzz around the nucleus in a sort of cloud or field and are nearly impossible to track. So, while the electrons themselves only account for a tiny portion of the atom, the field in which they are found makes up almost all of the atom's volume. Because of this, atoms are almost entirely empty space.

That means, in turn, all matter is almost entirely empty space. (Yeah, whoa!) Look at your hand. It seems solid enough, but on a microscopic level it is made up mostly of empty space. Think of the biggest, heaviest, most solid thing you can imagine. That thing, whatever it is, is made almost entirely of empty space. It doesn't matter whether an object is heavy or light, big or small. If you could look at its atoms, you would find it is mostly made of nothing at all!

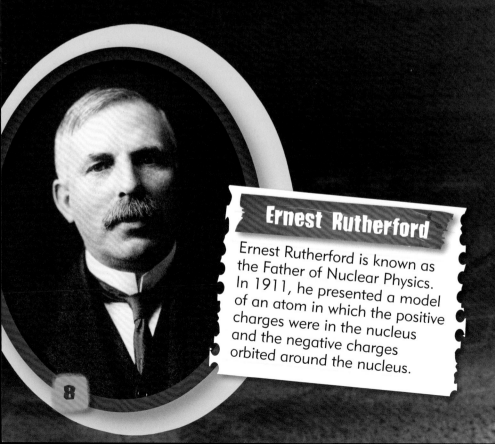

Ernest Rutherford

Ernest Rutherford is known as the Father of Nuclear Physics. In 1911, he presented a model of an atom in which the positive charges were in the nucleus and the negative charges orbited around the nucleus.

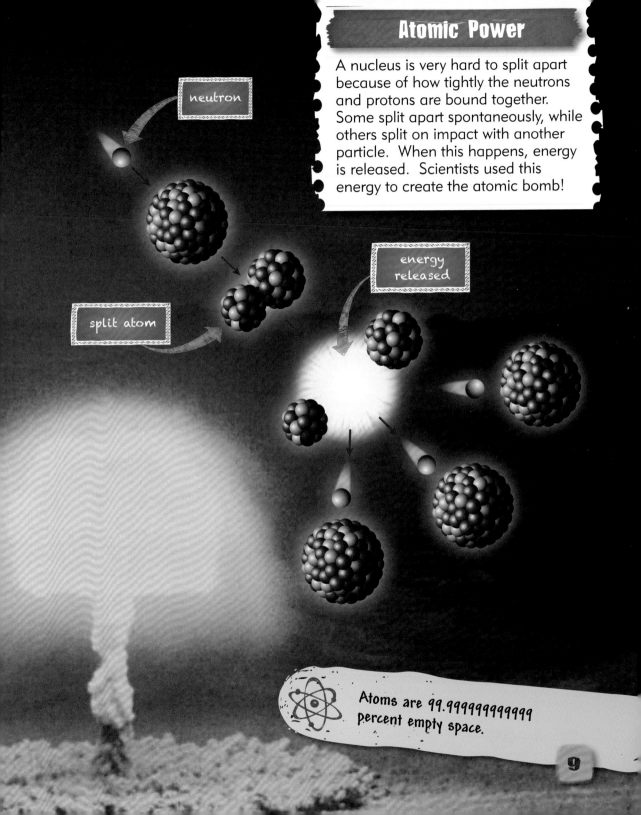

Atomic Power

A nucleus is very hard to split apart because of how tightly the neutrons and protons are bound together. Some split apart spontaneously, while others split on impact with another particle. When this happens, energy is released. Scientists used this energy to create the atomic bomb!

neutron

energy released

split atom

Atoms are 99.999999999 percent empty space.

Opposites Attract

Subatomic particles make up an atom. But these tiny pieces have another important role. They have electric charges. Electrons have a negative charge, protons have a positive charge, and neutrons are neutral. They have no charge at all.

Each charged particle interacts with other particles in certain ways. They work just like magnets. Since protons have a positive charge, they repel, or push away, other protons. Electrons also repel other electrons. But since protons and electrons have opposite charges, they are attracted to each other. Because neutrons do not have a charge, they neither attract nor repel other particles.

The nucleus of an atom is made up of protons and neutrons. So, the nucleus has a positive charge. Since electrons are negatively charged, they are attracted to the nucleus. This pull holds the electron cloud in place.

Even though they are not even close to the same size, electrons and protons have charges of equal strength. Atoms usually have a neutral overall charge. In order for this to be true, atoms must have an equal number of protons and electrons. If you know how many protons an atom has, then you also know how many electrons it probably has.

A Very Strong Force

Why don't protons in the nucleus push away from one another, breaking the atom apart? Protons and neutrons are bound tightly together in the nucleus. The force holding them together is stronger than the force pushing them apart. Logically, this force is called the *strong force*!

The strong force is 1,038 times stronger than gravity on Earth.

Elements

Atoms can combine in a variety of ways. A substance composed only of the same type of atom is called an **element**. For example, iron is an element. All of the atoms in pure iron are iron atoms.

There are many types of elements, each with different properties. Some elements, such as mercury, are liquid at room temperature. Others, such as helium, are gases. Still others are solid, such as lead. Some conduct electricity and heat. Others do not. Elements can be many different colors. They can combine into different things. Some elements have a distinctive smell or taste.

Regardless of these properties, you can tell each type of element apart by the number of protons it has. That means that if you could add another proton to an atom, then it would be a different kind of atom altogether! Of course, doing that is quite difficult and requires a lot of energy. But the fact remains that what makes elements different are the number of protons.

13
Al
Aluminium
26.9815386

Shortening It Up

The names of elements can get quite long and are not always fun to write over and over again. No one wants to keep writing aluminium! So scientists use standard abbreviations, or **chemical symbols**, for each type of element. The symbols are one to three letters long, with the first letter always capitalized. They are usually composed of letters from the element's English or Latin name.

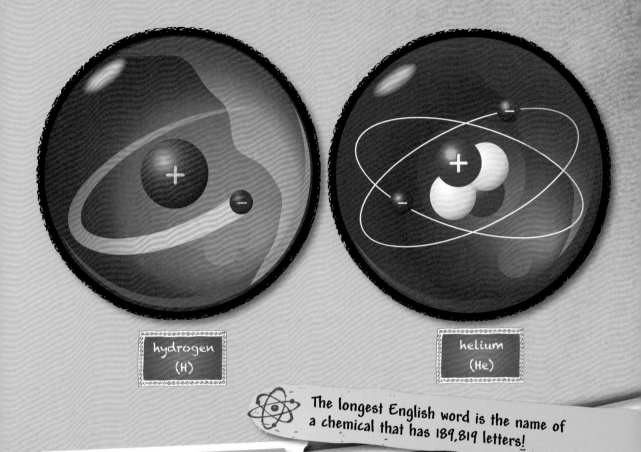

hydrogen
(H)

helium
(He)

The longest English word is the name of a chemical that has 189,819 letters!

Useful Elements

When you go to a water park or swim in a pool, you will probably notice that the water has a strong odor. You're smelling chlorine. Chlorine is a useful element that is commonly used as a disinfectant. Pouring the right amount of chlorine in pool water will keep the water clean. Chlorine is also used in bleach to clean clothes and dirty toilets.

Au
96.97

80

Hg
200.5

Electron Shells

Electrons don't just buzz around randomly. They occupy different energy levels, or shells, of an atom. A certain number of electrons fits into each shell. When one shell is full, electrons start filling up the next shell. A full shell is very stable and "wants" to stay the way it is. But an incomplete shell is not stable at all. The shells "want" to either be full or empty. The outermost shell is called the **valence shell**.

Protons and neutrons don't change much in their compact nucleus. But electrons can easily jump from atom to atom. When the valence shell of an atom is not full, the atom tries to become full. It may do this by giving its electrons away to other nearby atoms, or it may take electrons from other atoms. It may also share electrons with neighboring atoms.

The number of valence electrons in an atom controls how reactive an element is. The number also determines the types of elements it will react with and how they will react. This means that how an atom acts is based almost entirely on the number of valence electrons it has.

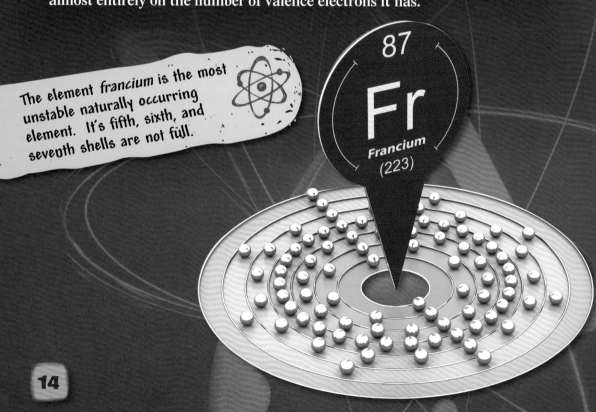

The element francium is the most unstable naturally occurring element. It's fifth, sixth, and seventh shells are not full.

87
Fr
Francium
(223)

Filling the Shells

Electrons always fill their shells in a precise way. The chart below shows how many electrons each shell can hold.

Shell	Number of Electrons	Shell Letter
1	2	K
2	8	L
3	18	M
4	32	N
5	50	O
6	72	P
7	98	Q

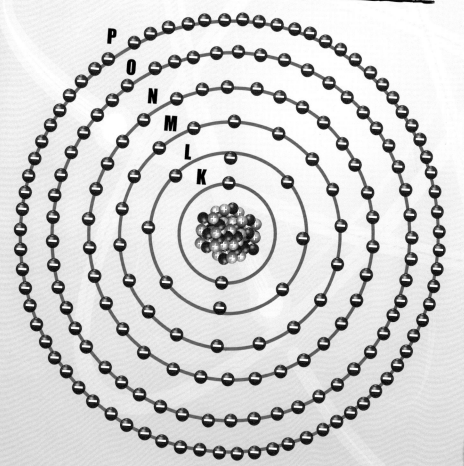

15

Molecules and Reactions

Elements that have an incomplete valance shell are very reactive. But what does that mean?

When atoms react with one or more other atoms, they join together. A set of joined atoms is a **molecule**. A molecule can be made of the same kind of atoms, making it an element, or it can be made up of different kinds of atoms, making it a **compound**. A compound often has very different properties from the elements that made it. For example, pure water is a compound. It is made of hydrogen and oxygen. When two hydrogen atoms and one oxygen atom come together with enough energy, they combine to form a water molecule. Hydrogen and oxygen are both colorless gases at room temperature. But as you know, water is a liquid at room temperature. Oxygen won't turn to liquid until it reaches a chilly -219° Celsius (-362° Fahrenheit) and hydrogen at -259°C (-434°F). Imagine if it were cold enough to have liquid oxygen raining out of the sky!

Very Unstable

Some elements are so reactive that they are not found in their pure states in nature. Just how reactive are we talking here? Sodium is very reactive. It will react with oxygen in the air. Sodium also reacts with water and, if the temperature is right, it can actually catch fire.

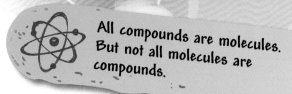

All compounds are molecules. But not all molecules are compounds.

There are millions of compounds known today. And more are always being discovered. Not all atoms can react with one another, though. It all comes down, once again, to the arrangement of their electron shells.

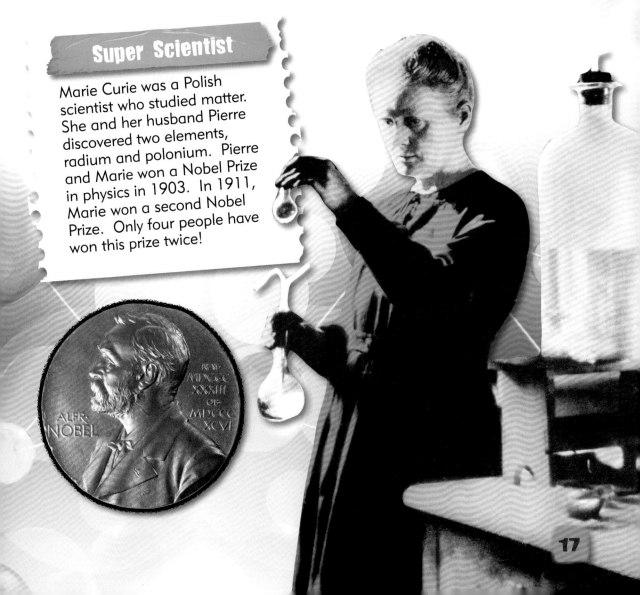

Types of Bonds

In order for two or more atoms to bond, or join together, they must physically meet. They also need to be compatible. This means they must have the right properties to create a reaction. In addition, they need energy to form the bond. If these requirements are not met, then no reaction will occur.

Atoms "want" to be as stable as possible. Unstable atoms usually bond in an attempt to complete their valence shells. There are different ways that two or more atoms can bond.

One way is through a **covalent bond.** Covalent bonds form when two of the same or similar atoms share electrons between them. To do this, they join valence shells. A covalent bond is usually formed between two nonmetals.

Doubling Up

Atoms can create a double bond. A double bond is when two atoms bond with each other twice. When both atoms are missing two electrons, they can fill each of those missing spots and create two bonds. Carbon is the most common element to form this type of bond.

Some elements, such as hydrogen, will form covalent bonds with themselves. They do this if there are no other elements to react with. These elements are called **diatomic**. *Diatom* means "two atoms." These atoms are naturally found in sets of two. Hydrogen, oxygen, fluorine and chlorine are all examples of diatomic elements.

Hydrogen is the most common naturally occurring diatomic molecule in the universe.

No Fair!

Atoms don't always play nicely. If atoms have different charges, then they might share their electrons unequally. One atom might hog the electron. Oxygen tends to hog electrons, giving it a negative charge. When hydrogen bonds with oxygen, the positive and negative charges attract, forming water.

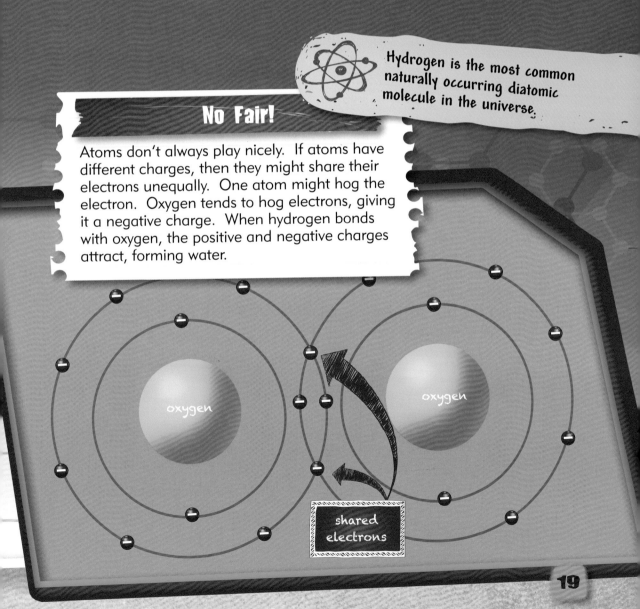

oxygen

oxygen

shared electrons

Another kind of bond is an **ionic bond**. An ionic bond forms between different types of atoms. In fact, ionic bonds usually form between metals and nonmetals.

An ionic bond is formed when one or more atoms take electrons from another atom to fill their valence shells. This creates charged **ions** because the numbers of electrons and protons in each atom do not match. For example, sodium has one electron in its valence shell. Chlorine has seven electrons in its valence shell. The sodium wants to give up an electron. And the chlorine wants to gain one to fill its outer shell. So, the electron from sodium jumps over and fills chlorine's shell. Now the sodium has a positive charge because it has more protons than electrons. And chlorine now has a negative charge because it has more electrons than protons. These two atoms are called *ions* because they have a charge. Since opposites attract, the ions come together and form an ionic bond. This forms a new molecule called *sodium chloride*—also known as table salt!

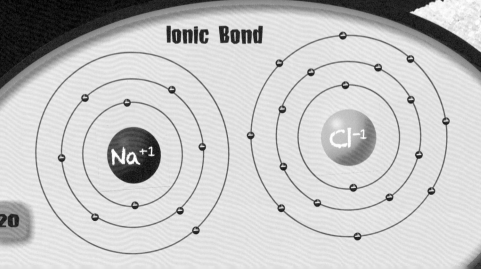

Ionic Bond

Na^{+1} Cl^{-1}

Ordinary Table Salt

Pure sodium is a silvery metal that is soft enough to cut with your ruler. But don't get it wet! It pops and fizzes when it touches water. Chlorine is a poisonous green gas. But put them together, and you have table salt!

Sodium reacts with water.

sodium

Metals vs Nonmetals

Metals and nonmetals have many differences.

Metals

- one to three valence electrons
- lose valence electrons easily
- good conductors
- metallic, shiny
- dense
- usually solid at room temperature
- melt at high temperatures
- easily bent into shapes
- examples: silver (Ag), gold (Au), platinum (Pt), potassium (K)

Nonmetals

- four to eight valence electrons
- gain or share valence electrons easily
- poor conductors
- dull, transparent
- low density
- solid, liquid, or gas at room temperature
- melt at low temperatures
- cannot change shape easily
- examples: hydrogen (H), carbon (C), nitrogen (N), oxygen (O)

Periodic Table of Elements

The periodic table of elements is a chart that organizes elements based on their properties. It can be very useful in understanding the relationships between different elements. The table is arranged in rows and columns. The rows are called *periods*. This is where the periodic table gets its name. The columns are called *groups*. The elements in each period are arranged by size. The elements in each group are sorted by property.

The periodic table organizes all the known elements.

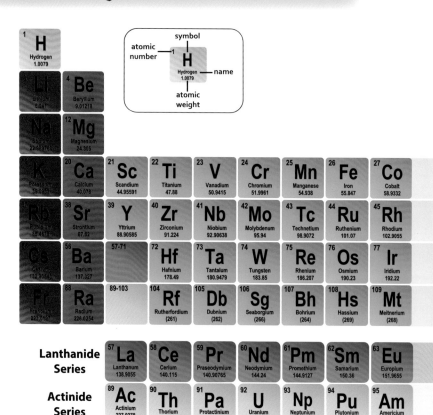

Each element is represented as a labeled square. Typically, at least three things are present. Each box will show the element's **atomic number** (how many protons it has), name, and chemical symbol. Most tables also use colors to show groups of elements that have something in common. All metals may be one color or texture. All nonmetals may be another. For instance, on this chart, the elements are sorted by color. The squares may also include a number that describes the mass or weight of the element. Chemists use this information to figure out how substances will react.

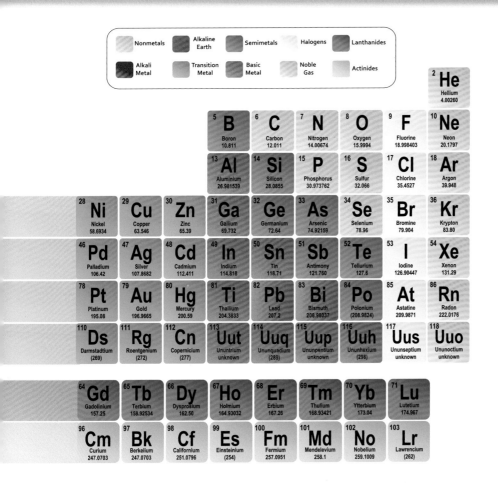

The Specifics

To better explain how this works, let's look at just one element—potassium. Potassium is a soft, silvery-white metal. Like pure sodium, it can be cut with a ruler or butter knife. Potassium is number 19 on the periodic table. This is also its atomic number. So we know that potassium has 19 protons in its nucleus. Its atomic weight is 39. This means that one atom of potassium weighs 39 atomic units. You might notice that the weight listed below is not exactly 39. This is because some potassium atoms are slightly heavier.

Potassium's chemical symbol is K. This may not look like it should stand for potassium, but it's because potassium's Latin name, *kalium*, begins with the letter *K*.

Potassium is in the fourth period of the periodic table, which means that it has four electron shells. It is also in the first group of the periodic table, which means that it is extremely reactive. In fact, it explodes when it touches water! Because of this, pure potassium is not found in nature. But it is found in many different compounds. Some potassium compounds are found in foods such as bananas and are very good for your body.

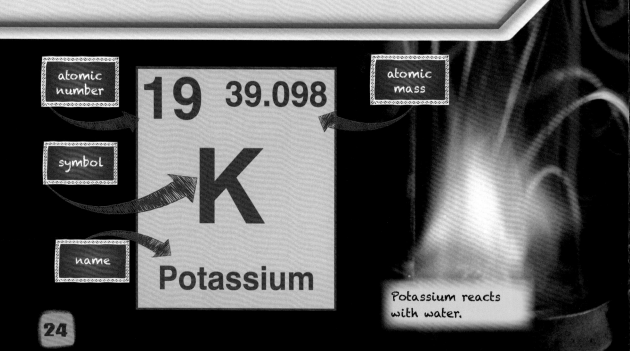

atomic number

atomic mass

19 39.098

symbol

K

name

Potassium

Potassium reacts with water.

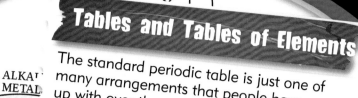

The standard periodic table is just one of many arrangements that people have come up with over the years. There are some arranged in spirals or circles. There are even three-dimensional models. The standard table is used most because it is simple.

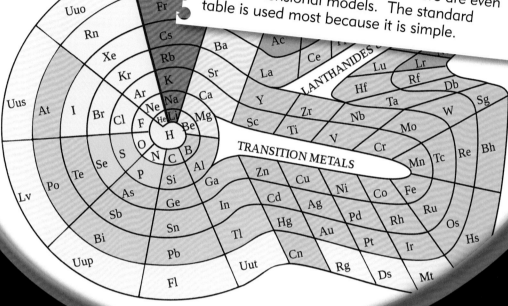

PERIODIC DIVIDE

NOBLE GASES

ALKALI METALS

NANTHANIDES

TRANSITION METALS

Creator of the Table

Dmitri Mendeléev (DMYEE-tryee men-dl-EY-uhf) created the periodic table we use today. He put elements in rows and columns by their atomic weight. But his genius idea was to leave gaps in the table. He predicted where undiscovered elements might be in the table. He guessed their properties based on their positions. Later, scientists proved his predictions were correct!

Not Just Bubbling Beakers!

Sometimes people like to say that food or products are bad because they have "chemicals" in them. But chemistry is the study of matter and how it interacts. So, "chemicals" are anything and everything that's made of matter. In short, everything is made of chemicals! It's true—some chemicals can be harmful. But if you understand their properties, you can know how to interact with them safely.

By studying matter and how it acts, we can make predictions about the world. We know what will happen if certain things are mixed together. We can also make changes to the world. Many of the products that exist today are a result of people studying matter. Chemists have learned how to make medicine that help treat diseases. And they have learned how to make plastics that are strong and light enough to build space shuttles! By learning more about the matter that surrounds us, we can find new ways to solve many problems.

People live longer today because of our knowledge about elements and how they react. This helps chemists make medicine that saves lives.

Accidental Discovery

Artificial sweeteners were discovered by accident in 1879. Constantine Fahlberg had been in his lab trying to make new food preservatives. He forgot to wash his hands, and one of the chemicals remained on his skin. At dinner that evening, he noticed that his dinner roll tasted sweeter than usual. Luckily, the chemical didn't kill him! Instead, he made an exciting discovery.

Think Like a Scientist

How can you create a chemical reaction? Experiment and find out!

What to Get

- $\frac{1}{2}$ cup hydrogen peroxide
- $\frac{1}{2}$ cup warm water
- 1 packet dry yeast
- 1 tablespoon liquid dish soap
- clean, plastic water bottle
- food coloring
- funnel
- safety goggles
- tray

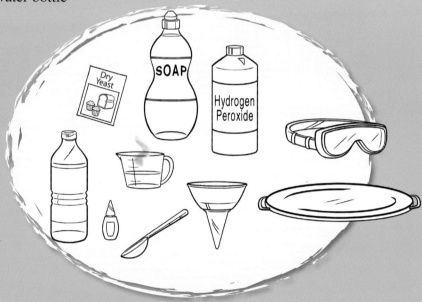

What to Do

1 Put on the safety goggles. Dissolve one packet of dry yeast in warm water and set it aside.

2 Add a squirt of dish soap into the bottle on the tray.

3 Put the funnel in the bottle opening. Carefully pour in the hydrogen peroxide. Add three drops of food coloring.

4 Swish the bottle around to mix the contents.

5 Add the dissolved yeast to the bottle and remove the funnel. What do you observe? Gently touch the side of the bottle. What do you feel?

Glossary

atomic number—the number of protons contained in the nucleus of an atom

chemical symbols—abbreviations for chemical elements, often derived from Latin names

compound—a substance made of two or more types of atoms bonded together

covalent bond—a chemical bond in which atoms share two or more electrons

diatomic—consisting of two atoms

electrons—negatively charged particles in an atom

element—a basic substance that is made of atoms of only one kind and cannot be separated by ordinary chemical means into simpler substances

ionic bond—a chemical bond formed between oppositely chargd ions

ions—atoms with a charge

mass—the amount of matter an object contains

molecule—the smallest possible amount of a particular substance

neutrons—particles that have neutral charges and are part of the nucleus of an atom

nucleus—the center of the atom that contains protons and neutrons

protons—particles that have positive charges and are part of the nucleus of an atom

valence shell—the outermost electron shell of an atom

Index

55.845   26

Fe

Iron

Matter Is Everywhere

Search your home for matter. Find 10 household items. Make a chart by listing each item. Organize the list based on properties. What kind of material is each item made of? What is its purpose? Why does it work? What else can you observe?